THE
PROFIT
PATTERN

The Top 10 Tools to Transform Your Business,
Drive Performance, Empower Your People,
Accelerate Productivity and Profitability

by

JOHN MAUTNER

Only 33% of all business owners take strategic and
tactical action when growing their businesses-- access
the The Profit Pattern Application Guide by emailing
proof of purchase to bonus@TheProfitPattern.com and
we'll send you our 50+ page guide that walks you
through the action steps, chapter by chapter, to improve
your bottom line.

To access further resources inside our membership site
that will transform your business, drive performance,
empower your people, accelerate productivity and
profitability visit www.TheProfitPattern.com/Bonus

DEDICATION

To my children, Connor and Rachel,
who always tell me, "You're doing a great job."

To JoAnn Becker who help me realize
the power of patterns

To Greg Huebner and Rick Connor
who have helped me grow COSi.

To all our clients who are the most amazing people ever,
it's an honor to be your coach

To my family and friends,
thanks for your help and love.

To you, yes you, as you read this book,
I hope you become more success as a result.

CONTENTS

"Small business isn't for the faint of heart.
It's for the brave, the patient and the persistent.
It's for the overcomer."

–Unknown

INTRODUCTION

My Story
Could Be Yours

For some people, when they first start imagining their dream life, being their own boss would be at the top of their list. Many of us long to be successful, financially independent, and in charge of our own lives and so we invest time and resources into building a business with the intention that it will not only support our lifestyles, but also that of our family, employees, suppliers, customers and communities for generations into the future. There are over twenty-eight million small businesses in the United States today - each of these small businesses has its own unique set of goals, problems, people and products – but each was started with the intention of building something great.

Maybe this is why you started your own company. You wanted to build a company that would allow you to live the life you've always dreamed about, you wanted to build something great that you and your employees could be proud to work on each day, or you wanted to build something for future generations to enjoy and admire. Those strong dreams we have in the early days are the ones that fuel all the long nights and tough times... but how long do those dreams last?

Unfortunately, there are millions of businesses underperforming right now in the United States. These small to midsized businesses are not growing, they aren't profitable and they aren't fulfilling the dreams and goals of the owners that started and sacrificed so much to get them up and running. I call this space, the difference from "where my business is" to "where I want my business to be," the **disappointment gap**.

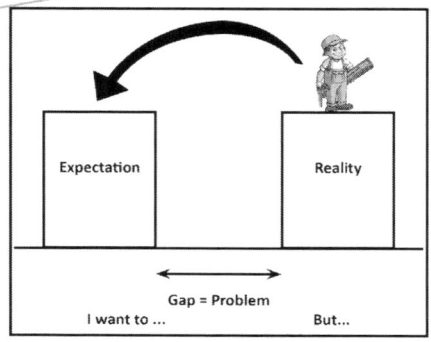

The disappointment gap is that empty feeling you get in your gut when you are staring at your bank account thinking, "How did we get here? Where did all the money go? How am I going to make ends meet?"

The disappointment gap is going home at the end of a long day, completely exhausted, but when it's finally time to go to sleep – you end up staring at your bedroom ceiling throughout the night with the constant stream of every problem your company has running through your head. How will we make our weekly payroll? How can we pay vendors who want money now? How will we deal with employees who don't give their best efforts... what about our demanding and difficult customers?

The disappointment gap is the pile of unopened bills you have in your top desk drawer. The ones that you can't bear to open because you know you don't have the money to pay them. So, for now, they seem like they are doing less damage as long as you can pretend they don't exist.

At some point, the disappointment gap is so wide, and the pain of 'maintaining appearances' to keep your company afloat so painful, that it feels like the best solution is throwing in the towel. At least then the bleeding will stop and you won't be dealing with all the problems that you are currently experiencing.

If this sounds familiar, I want you to know that you are not alone. There are millions of people who are going through this at the same time you are going through it.

If this sounds familiar, I want to make you a promise. There is help to be had.

You don't have to feel this way about your business, it can be saved, it can be turned around and you already have all the tools and resources that you need to get it done. And, if you're willing to take a positive attitude (or at least consider the possibility that you CAN get back to your dream business), this book will help by providing you with The Top 10 Tools that you can use to improve your business immediately, no matter if you are deep in the red or want to get further into the black.

Sadly, far too many small business owners will never realize their true potential and turn their business around into something amazing — not because they aren't smart enough, or because they didn't have the right resources — and certainly not because their business was actually doomed to failure. Most businesses that end in fail, file for bankruptcy and close down because the owner wasn't able or willing to admit that there was a real problem.

By identifying and admitting that there is a problem and that there is a disappointment gap in the first place is the first step toward success and to admit that fact to yourself, already puts you so far ahead of the curve — and I have every confidence that you'll be able to take action and begin making astounding changes in your business within the next 30 days.

The loss of your business would be devastating on many levels. It's bad for your heart, your soul, your family, your finances and for that of your employees. It's bad for the local and national economy and it's bad for your customers and vendors.

It doesn't have to happen and most of the time it should have never happened. But it does every day because ownership could not admit there are real problems and as a result were much too slow to react and suddenly it's too late.

I fix businesses. I am a coach, not a consultant. I walk into a company's headquarters with very little knowledge of how they really do things because, I have not worked there. So how could I really know what needs to be fixed to drive profitable growth faster. I may know the basics, but compared to the people who have worked there for years or even decades, I know nothing. So, how do I manage to help hundreds of businesses turn around and grow their entire business?

My unique approach is to harness the deep technical knowledge of the people already invested in the business (employees, vendors, customers) and I ask them very specific, very directed questions about the company's problems, challenges, opportunities and possible solutions. In the next ten chapters I'll teach you what I have discovered about a strange pattern – The Profit Pattern - that I discovered by working with over 4,000 business leaders.

While every business is unique and different, I looked back at the past 100 different companies in many different industries that I coached. Each had an average of one hundred problems their team of people identified. That's 10,000 problems identified! Then, when I asked their people what their top ten most important problems to fix were – across the board, ten particular opportunities popped up again and again like a broken record repeating itself over and over, amazingly, all these different companies all had the same top 10 problems, that if fixed, would significantly grow the top and bottom lines and get the business growing faster. That's why each of the following ten chapters is a particular "problem scope" that we're going to use as a framework for asking the important questions that will get you to the root of your company's problems (and then to the solution as well!).

I look forward to sharing The Top 10 Tools you can use to accelerate profitability, performance and productivity with you. If you enact these 10 proven tips and techniques I share with you throughout this book, I have no doubt that The Profit Pattern will have a positive impact on your business success now and into the future. So, what are the Top 10 problems that are the common denominators that over 4,000 owners, managers and employees all share?

- No Formal Sales Process
- Inconsistent Quality
- Lack of Standard Operating Procedures
- Scheduling Problems
- Poor Inventory Management
- Estimating/Bidding Errors
- Tight Cash Flow
- Lack of proper Project Management
- Communication Challenges
- Lack of innovation

To download a mini-report on the
TOP 10 Problems faced by thousands
of business leaders visit:
www.theprofitpattern.com/bonus
or Text PROFIT to 58885
to receive a PDF that defines each of the
problems and will allow you to further
discover if your business shares these
company killers.

"Many of life's failures are people who did not realize how close they were to success when they gave up."

–Thomas Edison

CHAPTER 1

What Does a Big Mac and an F-15 Have in Common?

You might be wondering exactly how someone started and built one of the 500 fastest growing companies in America. For me, it started with a college degree in accounting and finance. Really! After receiving my degree, I went to work in Corporate America and I lasted about a year before I realized that I could stay and retire from a cushy, but soul-crushing, job in twenty or thirty years or I could pursue my dreams of being an entrepreneur. I think I had my mid-life crisis at 26.

To say that my family wasn't exactly supportive would be

an understatement. The day after I got married and told my wife, friends and family that I was quitting my job because I had a dream of opening up a cinnamon roasted almond nut cart and someday have these carts all around the entire world – my family responded with something like, "Maybe that's not the best idea... we think you should reconsider" They basically thought I was nuts (pun intended).

But I was in my mid-twenties and I thought I had this amazing idea that I had to at least try and realized if I did not and someone else had the idea, how stupid I would feel if someone made this idea a success. So, I quit my job, moved from Hilton Head Island, South Carolina (a beautiful golf course community) and drove to Florida in my old pickup truck and a copper kettle. I was so positive that I would set the world on fire.

My first stop was in a small downtown district of Orlando called Church Street Station, where I parked my truck and walked into the mall manager's office and said, "Hey, I sell cinnamon roasted nuts made fresh in a copper kettle and I'm looking for a location." The manager decided to give me a shot and I was in business. I built a cart around the copper kettle, I got an umbrella and began working 80 hours a week in the mall. Within six months, I was practically bankrupt.

Not the most auspicious start to my world domination vis-a-vis roasted almond carts, but whatever it was that made me believe that this was a great idea wasn't fading. I knew that my roasted nut carts were great, I just didn't know why they weren't selling.

My family and friends of course by this time were ripe with advice. "Maybe you can get your old job back?" Sales were less than $100 per day, the mall manager kept asking me to pay the rent as I was 3 months late and I was down to my last $300 and I needed to do something fast. I used the process of elimination to determine what the real problem was. Was my product bad? Nope. Did I give poor service? Nope. Is the cart ugly? Nope. Was my hair parted on the wrong side of my head? Nope. I eliminated everything that could be the problem and reduced it down to 1 issue. The location was the problem.

Orlando had just opened a brand new sports arena for the new team the NBA Orlando Magic. I called the food services director at the arena who told me to send over a brochure and a sample, but knowing my product – which is half about the freshness and seeing them being roasted and the smell of cinnamon and sugar filling the air...well, it just doesn't hold up the same idea if the product is a day old by the time the food service director has a chance to sample it - I responded, "I'm going to be in the neighborhood tomorrow morning, can I just stop by and drop it off?" He said "sure kid come on over at 9am". I knew I only had one shot to impress him.

The next morning, I packed up my roasted nut cart from the mall location and put it in the back of the same old pickup truck and drove it over to the loading dock behind the Orlando Arena. I set the flame beneath the copper kettle and started adding the ingredients. The smell was amazing and people from inside the stadium started walking out, smelling these cinnamon roasted almonds, including the food director. He took a look at it and said, "You start tomorrow."

The next night, Magic of Orlando opened with 22,000 people in the stadium… I prepared for 3 hours, cooking and roasting almonds, making sure I had a few hundred bags ready to go and within about ten minutes I was completely sold out. The rest of the evening I did my best just to try and keep up. Within three months I had saved up enough to purchase another cart for the other side of the arena — but since I couldn't be in two places at once, I had to work at creating a process that another person could be trained to follow. I had two locations, each completely sold out every night. I thought that there was still more room for maximizing the sales potential of that one location, so I talked the food director into letting us hire college students to walk up and down the stands selling product. Now I was back in business and profitable with positive cash flow.

About the same time, Universal Studios opened up their brand new huge theme park, I called the food services director and he told me, "Hey kid, why don't you send me a brochure and a sample?"

I (again) told him that I would be in the area and could I just drop it off in the morning. The next morning, I wheeled my cart into this huge boardroom and was roasting almonds — suddenly, the entire staff started walking in as did the food service director. He gave me a thirty-day test because I created an experience that was very impactful.

The first month in the park, my little cart did $100,000 in sales and I could barely make the nuts fast enough, I am talking 110% production, pedal to the metal every day. I had found the 'secret sauce' – it wasn't me (or how I was parting my hair, I had wondered...), it was that customers who were going to parks and arenas were already spending $10 for a hot dog and $7 for a beer so, spending $3 for a bag of roasted nuts didn't seem to impact their wallets. That was going to be my niche. I began contacting other theme parks, Epcot, MGM, Magic Kingdom and they were receptive because of how well I was selling at their largest competitor. Within a year we did well over a million dollars in sales.

The visibility in these parks led to amazing opportunities and great publicity because millions of people from all around the world visited them – we even made roasted nuts for President's Bill Clinton's inaugural dinners and I started getting news articles about the company from all across the country. People from all over the world would be standing in line at my roasted nut carts and every day several people would ask how they could purchase their own cart and be in business just like me.

I had to build a system that allowed for us to open carts around the world, all with the same level of quality and product, processes, procedures, training, checklists, how to clean the equipment and how to open a location, etc. Each cart was its own little roasted-nut factory and I had to build a system that allowed different locations to open anywhere, every where and be successful.

Within six years of opening the first cart, the company became one of Inc. Magazine's 500 fastest growing companies in America – from having my last $300 in my pocket to a 100-million-dollar system-wide sales with locations in stadiums, theme parks, arenas and special events all around the world. So my strong vision became a reality because I believed it could and nothing was going to stop me as long as I believed anything is possible. The people I met, places I have been, things I experienced were sometimes surreal. I can tell you, the dream is good but the reality is 100 times better.

When I decided to sell my company, some of the same people who questioned why I had started it started asking why I would sell it when it was doing so well. Selling roasted nuts is fine, but it's not going to change anyone's life in a meaningful way. People were always asking me, "How did you build such a profitable high growth company and can you show me?" I said" I really don't know how I did it, I was just doing my thing, let me get back to you on that"

So I decided to really do something meaningful and help fellow business owners reach their dreams. I took a year off and deconstructed everything I had done over the past 6 years – how I went from a kettle in the back of my old pickup truck to an award winning multi-million-dollar company. I started at the beginning and worked diligently on identifying the tools, the techniques and ultimately the mindset that got me from point A to point B. I developed a four-step system called the Cycle of Success and I used that system to teach and coach companies for the past fifteen years on how to build profitable, high-growth companies. My clients have made millions from what I have taught them and many have become millionaires are a result. I think I am "the millionaire maker".

Coaching fellow entrepreneurs to realize their dreams and trying to make this world a little better, became my mission. I had fallen on my face many times. I had learned the hard way by not listening to my gut, I had made many costly mistakes but, most importantly I kept going and going no matter what the situation. I had received a PhD from the "School of Hard Knocks" and I figured out how to work through many tough problems – and help other entrepreneurs who were faced with the same problems I faced (or even worse).

But, when I first walk into a meeting with an entrepreneur, I tell them that I can't help them. It seems counter-intuitive and they always look at me with wide eyes, like, 'So…. why are you here?' But, I explain that I'm like that expensive piece of workout equipment that people buy right around the New Year, when they make a resolution to lose twenty pounds and buy an exercise bike or treadmill, but within a month it's nothing more than a glorified towel rack. Working with me can be a lot like that, if you're not willing to put in the work on your end, be really focused and keep to your commitments, it will not work. So who can help you? You can help you.

That said, I have never met an entrepreneur that I couldn't help in some way be more successful. That's why after working with thousands of business owners, managers and employees, I still feel confident when I tell them if you work with me, if you commit to the process, I guarantee I can make your company better – I can help you save and grow the company that has been your life and your dream.

Total Quality Management (TQM)

- Total Quality Management, is an approach that extends beyond ordinary statistical quality control techniques and quality improvement methods
- TQM is only one of many acronyms used to label management systems that focus on quality
- CQI (continuous quality improvement)
- SQC (statistical quality control)
- QFD (quality function deployment)
- QIDW (quality in daily work)
- TQC (total quality control)
- TQM is an integrative philosophy of management for continuously improving the quality of products and processes

---

Case Study: Julie Savitt AMS Earth Movers

I'd like to tell you a story about one of my clients, Julie.

Julie's grandfather started a small trucking company that would deliver gravel to construction sites all around Chicago. Her father took it over from her grandfather and when her father retired, Julie and her husband ran it together.

Things began changing when Julie and her then-husband decided to get divorced. Sales slowed, customers quickly began leaving and the bills continued to pile up. By the time the divorce was finalized, Julie was finally clued into the fact that her now-ex-husband was going around to their clients and telling them that Julie's company was going out of business and that they should seek a new vendor to do business with. By the time their divorce was over, Julie's company was practically bankrupt and $600,000 in debt.

That's when Julie called me. We sat down and I asked her what she wanted to do with her company. She paused for a moment before looking me straight in the eye and said, "This company was started by my grandfather. This company is my legacy from him and I want to keep it alive. I'm willing to do what it takes and I more importantly want to show my kids that in tough times, you don't give up".

We took stock of the situation, trying to get a handle on the fact that customers were leaving, there was no money in the bank and the bills were all due – we started by immediately reconnecting with customers to assure them that the business wasn't going anywhere, but Julie's ex-husband had done a really great job of seeding doubt in their minds and it didn't turn the tides completely.

We sat down all ten of her employees and explained the situation – and everyone was on board. They wanted to keep their jobs, keep the company, so we figured out what needed to be done. We started the Voice of the People process and we asked what their ideas were – how could we increase efficiency, productivity, profitability... what can we do right now?

In two short hours we had over 100 great ideas that could

be immediately implemented to make the company better, we prioritized the list and over the next 30 days we started to conquer and divide. Everyone was given a specific task and they were dedicated and focused on making those things happen.

We went to each of Julie's vendors and were completely transparent — we told them the history and what was happening and guaranteed payment if they would work with her. Over the next twelve months, sales started to grow and expenses were being covered. Over the next five years, Julie won Entrepreneur of the Year, Woman Business Owner of the Year and several construction awards for high quality of service and safety. She now has a profitable five-million-dollar company, she will tell you that "we always have challenges and we are a work in process but, business and my life are better and my children learned an important life lesson".

For her, like for a lot of us, it is knowing that if in your darkest moments or hours you don't believe it can be done, then it probably can't. You have to rethink that thought process and start your changes there. The impossible is only impossible until you can find a way to make it happen. After all, the word impossible is spelled im-possible.

The Big Mac and an F15 Fighter Jet

What do a Big Mac and an F15 Fighter Jet have in common? I love asking my clients this question, I get a lot of interesting answers – like, "they will both kill you", "they both have lots of grease in them" "they both are really fast", all sorts of fun responses, but the answer I'm always looking for is that each of these things is made exactly the same way, every single time using a written standard operating procedure.

If you manufacture the F15 Fighter Jet differently each time and someone forgets to install some small nuts and bolts they were supposed to, well, maybe the landing gear will fall off and you'll have a major problem. Let's say there wasn't a procedure for creating a McDonald's burger, then the product isn't consistent. Right now you can go to a McDonald's in New York City and order a Big Mac and go to North Carolina and order a Big Mac and you will get an almost identical burger.

The customer experience is therefore completely consistent from one burger or one fighter jet to the next. Procedures are critical for any company that wants to improve quality and profitability quickly with a higher level of consistency.

One of the Top 10 I see all the time is the lack of Standard Operating Procedures. Procedures are everywhere if you think about it. You don't just jump into an F15 and take off the way you want to (or you might, but, I don't think you'll be flying again anytime soon). The Navy has a procedure all pilots must follow, pre-flight checklists, take off, landings, everything is recorded and systematized so that they can have the fewest number of deviations from their expectations of what will happen.

Same thing with the Big Mac. Every McDonald's franchisee and employee is handed a rather large operations manual that details the building of every product McDonald's makes and exactly how to make them – down to the number of pickles that go onto each burger and how fast it should take to make the product.

I worked with a client in St. Louis, a bakery that specialized in making these amazing glazed donuts that they would sell to hotels and convention centers each morning. The night before, Toni would get the order and make the glazed donuts – he was the glazed donuts king. But, when Toni was tragically killed in an accident, the business was in a tailspin. No one knew how to make the donuts! Toni had all the intellectual property locked up in his head and when he passed, all of his knowledge, his entire long legacy, went with him.

Think about the intellectual property you have in your company – what are the ideas and experiences that the people of your company share by virtue of working within the organization? What if they leave or quit, would you be able to easily replace them or is that information gone forever?

One of the most successful things McDonald's has done with their "factory like" production – is that by systemizing the way the Big Mac was made; they are able to plug a new employee into any portion of the process without a lot of ramp up. It's not the people that make the burgers what they are, it's the process.

This allows McDonalds (and would allow your company) to have a complete training program, which promotes documentation – which then promotes accountability! I worked in a lot of fast food restaurants as a teenager, but back then I liked my French fries rather dark and extremely crispy – but that's not how the procedures were set up for French fries. They wanted them lighter and less crispy – so I was forced with the decision to follow the process or be out of a job, because the manager didn't have a choice but to enforce the procedures. It held me accountable to the needs of the business and not to my personal whims. Does your company have a clear set of procedures and are people being held accountable to always follow them, every day?

SOPs are everywhere. If they are not documented, they need to be documented or updated and utilized. I am not suggesting go out and write 900 standard operating procedures tomorrow, but I would suggest putting together a cross-functional team inside the company, get people from sales, marketing and production, accounting, whatever departments you have in the company. Put a cross-functional team together and put out this idea in the middle of the table, say what do we need to document? What are the procedures that we need to have that will be most important that are critical to our success? What are the procedures that need to be updated and what are the procedures that we have in place but people are not following? The sales person might say 'I need a procedure on how do I handle objections in the sales process', someone from accounting might say 'I think we need a procedure on making sure the time cards are filled out properly for everyone out in the field', the production person might say 'I think I need a procedure on how to set the machine up properly so everyone does it the same consistent way and we can all measure to make sure we get it done in 15 minutes versus ½ hour every time'.

The starting point is again to engage your people ask them what they are thinking. You might come up with 100, then I would say out of 100 what is the top 10 that we need to implement first?

Prioritize them based on impact to profitability, quality and performance for the company. That is the only way that one can really wrap their mind around it and get started, get everyone in the company to solicit their ideas on what needs to be documented, make a procedure around it and then prioritize that list because otherwise it is kind of mind numbing. I do not want you to begin by creating procedures that have a smaller impact on profitability of the company, I want you by starting to implement the most important procedures that will make a big difference. Come at it from the perspective where are the biggest root causal problems we are having right now? One might be we cannot get the orders shipped out fast enough. Why not? Because the root cause is that we are not getting machines set up quickly enough.

Benefits of SOP's

- Provide continual development of operations
- Improve of communication with employees
- Simplify new employee training
- Share experience knowledge and ideas

It is critical to get a company's SOPs documented. For the intellectual property, think about all the knowledge your people have and all the years of experience they have. You want to harvest all of that and document it so that you can keep it within the firm, which can enhance the value of your business.

The #1 Procedure Killer

I have an example of a construction company that I worked with that had a new procedure to get the trucks out the door earlier in the morning. They would have 100 trucks they needed to get out the door and it took about an hour. The more crews spend time in the yard the more we cannot spend billing our clients out in the field for doing electrical work.

The idea is how do we get the crews and trucks out faster in the morning, a team was assembled and they came up with some really innovative ways that they could get the trucks out the door faster in the mornings such as: restocking, loading and fueling the trucks at night. In fact, they were able to get it out the door faster by 25%, instead of it being an hour it was now 45 minutes resulting in 25% more billing and production time.

Guess who appeared when the procedures were implemented to the crews? Well it is what I call 'Angry Al, Debbie Downer, Stubborn Sam and Lazy Lisa', these are people that did not want to do it the new way and it became a critical issue. The number one killer of an SOP is: lack of enforcement and accountability. I really find it to be a shame when a beautiful new procedure is put into place and it works wonderfully and some oppose it. They found a great way to get the trucks out the door faster and it is going to benefit everyone inside the company and create a better customer experience. Yet people were resistant, they were saying "I have been loading and driving the truck for 10 years, I am an electrician, and I've got my truck and do not tell me what to do".

These sorts of conflicts arise when you begin instituting structure and procedures. I always say is takes 21 days and countdown from there – that's how long it takes to build a new habit within the company – so you have be tough and firm for 21 days. Letting them know that you are introducing these procedures to improve quality and customer experience. By explaining the importance or value to the bottom line, most people can understand the value of the change. But, you're still going to find one or two people who don't want to play by the new rules.

At this point, you have to be the manager of a McDonald's – either stand up for the procedure (if it's working, if it's not – that's a different discussion) and enforce it, or you back down. You have to back up your procedures or you'll lose all credibility.

The idea isn't to force another inane procedure down someone's throat – the procedure should make the person's job easier, faster, less stressful and more enjoyable. Sending it out there amongst your employees and asking them to try it for a month and then return with feedback for tweaking the system is a great way to overcome objections and to get employee buy-in.

But, if by all accounts, the new system is working better – and yet you still have one or two employees that will not get on board, my advice is to let them go work for your competitor. I don't want you to start firing people willy-nilly, but I want you to realize that your company is everything because of its people. Your people are the most critical part of your success – so the people you invite into your company are also extremely important (as are the people you allow to stay).

You want to be slow to hire, quick to fire anyone who, having been given the right training, procedures and motivation, is still unable (or worse, unwilling) to do their job with the right attitude. A few bad apples can spoil the whole bunch.

If I asked you to take a look at the bottom 10% of people in your company, ranking them based on two criteria – best attitude and best aptitude, if you took a look at the bottom

10% of people – I want you to estimate how much money you are spending or investing on their salaries, benefits and continued employment. These people are adding the least to your organization and may, in fact, be taking away from it.

Making sure that your system and procedures are in place means that you are ensuring that your company won't have any sacred cows (i.e. people who can't be fired, because they basically hold all the knowledge of how things work). You do not want to be held hostage by one employee – you want to promote and invest in employees with the right attitude and the right aptitude. And everyone else, like I said before, can go work for your competition.

Not sure how to create
your own dream team?
Download my tips on creating your own
10-person team and get them started
on brainstorming! Visit:
www.theprofitpattern.com/bonus
or Text *PROFIT* to 58885
to access it today.

"You know that if you can make a business get off the ground then you are absolutely capable of accomplishing anything in this world."

–Kristen Prescott

CHAPTER 2

The Voice of the People

Voice of the People - Discover What's Holding You Back

I don't know anything about a company when I walk in the door. Every company is unique and no one knows the company like the people who work inside that company – they have, sometimes, decades of experience and a deep technical knowledge of every inch of what makes that company function.

I think that if you hire a consultant and they walk in the door and start telling you that they know everything about your business, and start demanding changes from the get-go without really understanding how your company ticks, you should show them the door. That person will be wrong most of the time and they will create a ton of stress, fear and animosity amongst the people in your organization.

I start the process by pulling a cross-functional team of people from different areas of the company – different backgrounds, different positions, and different departments; I call this the "Voice of the People". I usually select a ten-person team (the dream team!) and begin working with them on discovering and defining what the problems and possible creative solutions are to the big speed bumps that are keeping the company from being its most profitable self.

All people want to be heard and feel like their opinions matter, and this is a great way to get employees to not only share their deep knowledge, but also get them to feel invested and engaged in the company's future growth.

We discuss and create on average, a long listing of 100 actionable ideas that can be implemented immediately to improve the company's standing – right away. Once we've identified a hundred actionable things the company can do, we prioritize them and work with the top ten most critical items and use my knowledge of best practices, team problem solving and systemization to rapidly implement the ideas across the company.

We create 4 – 6-person Tiger Teams of employees to

implement these top 10 actionable items and then create a new standard operating procedure that allows us to repeat a successful response over and over again.

This is a simple process that I've worked with hundreds of times, with great success, adding millions to the companies I have coached… but it all starts with the entrepreneur that is willing to fight.

One of the biggest struggles that a company can face is choosing and following the correct strategy for growing their business. It's not always easy to balance innovation with a "safe plan" for growth… While the need to grow is a great problem to have, growth for a company is fraught with challenges – the wrong decision could mean lost revenue, lost profit and lost time.

While growing my first company, we faced these challenges by innovating (making small or large incremental changes) to allow us to improve our sales, our processes, our training and most of all, our profits as people began noticing the roasted nut carts in theme parks or stadiums. People from around the world began approaching me, looking for a way to open a cart. We were faced with the same questions any business poised to grow faces: choosing the correct growth strategy for our company.

My primary goal from the beginning was to have carts around the world as fast as possible. Some locations were going to be company owned, while all other locations were through a licensing program I designed. We would sell a turnkey package including: a fully operational cinnamon roasted nut cart, help them find a great location and build their business with training and then sell the nuts, packaging and cinnamon glaze products to the licensees.

The second way for us to grow was to make a substantial investment back into the company to open up several new locations over the next year, so I decided to do both licensing carts and open more company-owned locations as the strategy.

At the time I had five profitable locations, working with Disney, Orlando Arena, Bob Carr Performing Arts Center and Universal Studios in Florida, so in order to reach my goal of opening several new locations in the US and in 20 countries. I wanted to open new location as fast as possible which put a tremendous amount of pressure and stress on my organization and on myself.

These stressors were what eventually made our company great. We were coming across problem after problem and it forced us to find solutions too! Over the course of 12 months, I had to train over 100 new employees, manage and deliver inventory needed for all the locations, ensure that we had the right supplies in place and that the quality of each location met my high standards.

The questions I kept asking myself was; how do we make sure that any customer could approach any of our locations anywhere is the world and purchase the same high quality product, with the same great customer experience? I decided to get the Voice Of The People. I did not know who the right way to move forward. So, I created a cross functional team of employees from all departments and asked them "what are our biggest problems?" "What are you thinking that can make a difference"? We brainstormed and we made a list of the Top 5 Problems we must deal with now is we are going to move forward. This was very exciting to everyone. The team felt empowered that I cared enough about their opinions.

Problem #1: Consistent, Quality Product

For someone who is as obsessed with quality and consistency as I am, roasted nut carts were enough to start a panic attack. With a cinnamon roasted nut cart, you are dealing with a copper kettle, very high heat, a hot gas flame, candy making techniques, lots of cinnamon and sugar – which means that you could ruin an entire batch of product if the temperature was even a few degrees too high or too low, or if you turned the machine off too soon, or if you let them cook a little too long.

Our big problem was finding out how we could make sure everyone was roasting a perfect batch of nuts, every time. We created written procedures and training manuals that broke down every step of the business for our new employees and licensees – everything from greeting a new customer to closing the cart in the evening. While this helped us to create a consistent product, we weren't able to create procedures for the problems we didn't know would exist, which led us to problem number two.

Problem #2: Cash Control

There is a certain amount of loss attributed to any new business, but training 100 new people in several different locations in the US and internationally in such a short amount of time meant that I was working with veritable strangers and the new licensees would have to trust to take cash from customers and make sure it made it to the register.

I trained the owner and manager of each cart on the procedures which is what made my initial carts so successful. They, in turn, would train the other employees, and when I opened up a company-owned location at a major theme park in Cincinnati, this cart was no different. Later, I noticed that the sales at this location were not growing as well as I would have liked, but I had dozens of other locations that were all having their own problems. Eventually it was brought to my attention that we were sending a lot of extra inventory to this location but, the revenues weren't matching and food cost was much higher than normal – and when I finally looked into it fully, I realized that our manager had stolen almost $30,000 in cash from the business.

This wasn't only a problem for me, but also for my partnership with the theme park that would make a percentage of our sales revenue. Hiring the wrong person didn't just affect my bottom line, it affected my entire business reputation and could have negatively affected my business' future growth.

We had a lot of great procedures that ensured great quality of product, but that didn't take into consideration possible theft because it hadn't originally been a problem we needed to consider. I had taken the plunge to reinvest a large sum of money into this business in order to expand rapidly – thinking that more business meant more money meant fewer problems. But in reality, that level of rapid growth was almost uncontrolled. We didn't know the problems we would be facing and so we didn't have a plan for what problems came with rapid growth and it almost put us out of business.

Problem #3: Growth Logistics

I consider Orlando, Florida an "international city" as they get over 30 million tourists each year from all over the globe. Because I had my carts in some of the most visible high traffic tourist locations in this area, I had a built-in marketing platform for sharing my business idea with the world. I placed a little sign on my cart saying that if someone was interested in the cart as a business opportunity they could call me to get more information.

I was approached by a huge real estate developer from Sao Paulo, Brazil. He was looking for a business opportunity for his wife, she loved the product and business model and they were both interested in bringing this product to Brazil. I licensed them to open 50 carts throughout Brazil over the next 3 years. After the initial excitement wore off, I had to figure out exactly how I would handle the logistics of being in Orlando and having carts in Brazil. How would we get suppliers for the cinnamon nut glaze, packaging and almonds? How would we ship carts or was it cheaper to have them made in Brazil? What about health code approvals? Did they even have almonds in Brazil? On top of that, Brazil was just one of the 20 other countries wanting to open locations at the same time.

How could I grow the business and have it make sense, no matter what country we were in? I believed that this was the key to exponential growth and that 30, 50, or even 100 carts were a part of my future so I poured money back into the company to fund that growth.

Problem #4: Finding My Niche

There are a lot more shopping malls in our country than sports stadiums and arenas and originally, my first cart location was within a shopping mall and I thought it was a great niche to develop my business in. Until I opened my first cart in a sports arena. Sales went crazy, I couldn't keep product in stock because sales were so good – and until then, I had thought that shopping malls were going to be my niche.

Here's why: shopping malls normally are open from 10 am – 9pm, the hours are huge, if you are standing at a nut cart for 10 hours a day, 7 days a week, that's a lot of hours just to be present, in addition to the time before the mall opens when I have to get the product, prepare the cart, pick up the almonds and all of the general business work. Some days I was excited I got to $100, but most days it was $30-$50. Imagine 6 months of just horrible sales, what does that do to you?

Then we opened our first cart in a sports arena – the hours were shorter (only 4 hours during events) and the audiences at those events were looking to purchase foods that were easily consumable in the stands. We pivoted our locations to the ones that created the largest revenues and then looked for similar spaces in terms of foot traffic, events, activities and people. We began looking at the best theme parks, stadiums and arenas in the world where the foot traffic could be in the tens of thousands in a single day as opposed to the steady stream of a much lighter traffic pattern as they have in malls.

Another benefit to us moving into the arena and theme park niche and out of the mall market was that we could really corner the market (because the niche was smaller but the market was larger!). Any time that you prove a business to be successful there will be people who copy and try and reproduce your efforts. You can't eliminate competition from the world, but you can try to limit it in your market niche. By working with large venues and concentrating our growth on cornering those markets and providing excellent experience for the customers and the location management, we were able to get a foothold early and eliminate the competition. When I first began, I didn't have any business entrepreneurial training, but I stayed focused on the big vision by focusing on what was working and by making consistent, but small improvements and then made sure that we were completely filling my niche as fast as possible.

Problem #5: Sales

Convincing food service directors and their stadiums, arenas and theme parks to give us a chance wasn't always easy. Some people were afraid that we'd end up stealing sales from other food categories or that we weren't going to provide a good customer experience for their patrons – losing them money and customers. It's never easy to convince someone to give you a chance on something new and different.

I thought if I could make the food service director happy he would tell a colleague and another colleague in another stadium and another arena. It's a small world in those industries. A good reputation was critical because we needed references to help convince the next skeptical food service director.

We hit a lot of roadblocks during our growth, a lot of struggles. I'd like to say that it was always easy to come up with a solution – but it wasn't. When I started my first location at the mall, there was time when I was down to my last $300 and it was a choice between reinvesting it into a failing (at the time) business – where common sense told me I should just quit and use that last $300 to sustain myself until I can find a job. I believe life will test you, testing how "bad do you want it". I realized the tougher the test, the greater the reward so, I did not give up, ever.

The question was whether it was the product that was bad ("Is it me? Is it the cart? Is my hair parted on the wrong side of my head?") and I think that's a point that a lot of entrepreneurs can understand and empathize with. Maybe you are at this point right now, you believed whole-heartedly in your business, you invested everything you had into it (and potentially a lot of money you didn't have) and you went after it – you did everything you think you were supposed to do and sales just aren't meeting your expectations (or your bills.)

People will tell you it's time to quit, it's time to raise the white flag and walk away with what little ego and money you have left. I've been there and I understand how demoralizing this point in your entrepreneurial life can be – you had such high expectations and now you don't know what to do. What worked for me, might work for you.

But you'll have to do what I did – and what's great is that what I did (asking questions, reevaluating the business and making tough decisions with a certainty that I just didn't have) can work for other businesses and it can work for yours.

If I had asked someone, prior to my success, if they would like to invest money in my business – the answer would have been, "I forbid you to put another dime into this thing! It's dead, let it die!" I was two weeks away from closing and losing everything down to my last $300. Something had to be done and it had to be done right away.

If you are at a similar crossroads in your business, it's time to take a good, hard look at your business and ask, what is wrong here? What is happening? What is going on? What can be better?

For me, it wasn't the product or the process, it was the location. I was trying to sell ice to Eskimos when I should have been selling it to sport fans and theme park attendees. Moving to arenas and theme parks was like making that key shift. And you can use the same process to find your ideal customers, too.

What's great about the questions that we ask and the

answers that we get is that they are both right under our noses. It's difficult to see them when we aren't looking for them, but the answers are all within your company.

I could have folded my business, walked away believing I was a failure and went through the rest of my life in quiet desperation... but I wanted it to succeed more than I wanted to be right. Once I gave up thinking I had all the right answers already, I was able to ask the right questions and get the correct answers to save my business, turn it around and become one of the fastest-growing companies in the country.

Since 2001, I've worked with thousands of business leaders, teaching them the techniques that I used to start and build the roasted nut company into one of the 500 fastest growing companies in the country (according to Inc. Magazine). Coaching business leaders, I have seen in excess of TEN THOUSAND complex problems, things that would destroy companies, I've coached over four thousand people on finding the answers to the right questions – and helping them rebuild their businesses into successes. In these ten thousand problems, I have yet to find one company that hasn't benefited, that hasn't been made better or more profitable from following the same strategies that I used to "fix" my own company from a failing cart in a shopping mall.

What problems are keeping your company
from being innovative?
Take a moment to stop reading
(yes, put the book down for a moment)
and visit:
www.theprofitpattern.com/bonus
or Text *PROFIT* to 58885
to access the ABC's of igniting
innovation within your organization.

"Nothing will work unless you do."

–Maya Angelou

C H A P T E R   3

Why Problems Always Seem to Start at the Top

D r. Guha was a doctor in India that dreamed of helping more people become medical doctors. The way the academic world works now, is that only about 10% of people who want to become a doctor are admitted to medical school…and Dr. Guha believed that the more people who were admitted the more people there would be out in the world helping people and helping save lives. So, in the early 2000s, he founded The St. James School of Medicine. They have a corporate office in Chicago, but their medical schools have campuses based in the Caribbean.

There are other established schools in the Caribbean, and there is also a lot of stigma in the medical industry around going offshore for medical school. The implication being that you couldn't make it into a traditional school in the United States so you had to go to a lower tier school and therefore were going to receive a lower tier education and become a lower tier doctor. Dr. Guha wanted to create a medical school that was both extremely rigorous and competitive – academically – but would meet the demand of the almost 90% of people who couldn't attend the typical U.S. based schools.

When he launched the medical school, he had about 100 students enrolled in the program – but he wasn't even breaking even. The capacity was for 500 students – they had the campuses, the facilities, the professors – but the seats weren't filled and yet the expenses were the same for 100 students and they would have been for 500.

When we met, we knew that part of the problem would be overcoming the social stigma about going to an offshore medical school, overcoming the perception that it was a low-quality education. We also had to resolve some problems that were happening within the organization, where Dr. Guha's daughter was running the day-to-day operations, but was constantly being overshadowed by her father – who would make decisions without her knowledge and basically going over her head.

We made a list and came up with the top ten things we could do to improve the company right away:

When we assembled people within the organization and asked them to focus on what real marketing things that they would need to do so that people knew this was a great way to get a quality education, we came up with a great list.

Using case studies, testimonials and sharing the campus experience of the quality of education students would get (while living on a beautiful island) didn't hurt. Explaining how students would get placed into rotations in the US hospitals upon graduation – so they knew they could go offshore to learn and come back to the United States to practice.

The team also noted that the messaging and branding were all outdated. The logo was something hand drawn by Dr. Guha himself, so from a strictly branding perspective, we had to make sure that all of our marketing materials reflected the level of professionalism that students could expect from a high-level medical school.

Next, we worked with leads – they were receiving upwards of 500 leads a week, but very few students were enrolling. Once we were able to identify the roadblocks that were keeping students from "pulling the trigger" – we built a system that helped potential students find financial aid, get immigration paperwork, passports and other documentation – these things were huge hurdles for someone who was unprepared to go to school offshore.

We were able to tweak the tuition model to make it a more attractive proposition for more students – which didn't hurt Dr. Guha's bottom line as enrollment improved.

That's when we started to gain traction – it didn't happen

overnight, but within six months, things started to come together. Enrollment numbers began to rise and we were ready for another team meeting. We gathered all the doctors and faculty and asked them how do we make this a better experience for students? We were given all sorts of suggestions... things like brighter colors in the classrooms to advanced training materials. We solicited this information so that students who attended became our biggest referrals.

As I mentioned, Dr. Guha's daughter Shirsha was working in the company as the Chief Operations Officer, running the day-to-day operations of the business. Everyone reported to her. What was happening though was that Dr. Guha was unable to step away from having control over the day to day aspects of the business. Not because he didn't trust his daughter, but because they didn't have a clear division of roles and responsibilities.

This caused a lot of expensive problems that impacted the business directly. We shifted Dr. Guha to being the CEO and being in charge of special projects while Shirsha was named the President and was in charge of the overall business. We also created a clearer hierarchy so that the business could run more smoothly (even if Shirsha was not available that particular day). With Dr. Guha able to concentrate on larger projects that could really move the organization forward and Shirsha reporting to him on a regular basis, both were happy as well as the entire organization. They were able to move forward and empower their people to do their jobs.

Without a clear organization structure, morale will be down, you (as the entrepreneur) will be stressed out, unable to leave the office (because nothing will get done!), and you'll always be so afraid that you don't have all the information or know what's going on that you won't be able to make clear decisions – let alone allow your team members to do the jobs you are paying them to do!

The idea that Dr. Guha had of empowering people to become doctors, ones that would never have been able to pursue their dreams otherwise, became a reality. He helped hundreds of doctors become successful in their fields, save lives and make the world a better place. All because one person focused on this dream and vision, looking inside their company to find the problem and empowering his people to help him get there.

I like to talk about Dr. Guha's success – because it wasn't just a professional success for him (and for his many graduates), it was a personal success as well. Like many small business owners, Dr. Guha wasn't exactly trained in medical school on how to run a business, so what happened to Dr. Guha happens to a lot of small business owners: they find themselves running a company without really knowing how to do so – and their lack of experience makes them more nervous, more controlling and more tight-fisted at the reins. Have you ever known anyone who you would've described as a control freak or a micro-manager? Do you know anyone who would describe you this way?

Chances are that if you are a micromanager, you might

not even know it. But, if any of the following sound familiar, you might just be a micromanager:

- You consider yourself a perfectionist, even of other people's work?
- You like to know (in minute detail) what every team member is working on?
- You prefer to be cc'ed on all emails?
- You want to keep your fingers in everything that is going on and prefer to have all decisions go through you?

Micromanaging may just seem like a perfectionist at work, but the financial problems associated with micromanaging can have a deep impact on your bottom line. A clear organizational structure is key to keeping yourself out of micromanaging, which will make sure that each of your team members has a very clear and very distinct idea of what their job is, what their role is within the organization and the impact that they make.

For many small businesses, the problems begin at the top – and the top is historically slow to change, so when the owner is a micromanager, it is basically stifling the entire company – which causes employees to feel untrusted, which causes dissatisfaction, which causes... well, it's a big cycle of negativity.

Letting go, if it's a small business owner that has held a chokehold on a business for too long, can change the entire company in a short period of time. I'm not saying that you need to lock yourself out of the office, but systematically moving the work, ownerships and decision-making abilities to the employees that you hired is a good first step.

When your people know that you believe in them, their entire demeanor and attitudes will change – and you'll finally be able to start enjoy working within your company.

Is the head of the company
a problem in your business?
(Worse yet, are you both the head
of your company AND the problem?)
Download this easy checklist that will help
you identify whether or not you are a cause
of issue and concern in your own company
(and some tips on correcting it!). Visit:
www.theprofitpattern.com/bonus
or Text PROFIT to 58885.

JOHN MAUTNER

"We are what we repeatedly do;
excellence then, is not an act but a habit."

–Aristotle

CHAPTER 4

Are You Growing, Plateauing or Slowing

One of the top ten that I see constantly is companies that struggle with sales. It always comes down to a few key issues that keep businesses from getting the sales that they are looking for. A lack of sales process can plague your company's top and bottom lines. One of the things we look at is the sales process – is there a clearly defined step by step process that allows all the salespeople to approach sales in a similar fashion? Is there a clearly defined problem that the customers are having that your salespeople are answering?

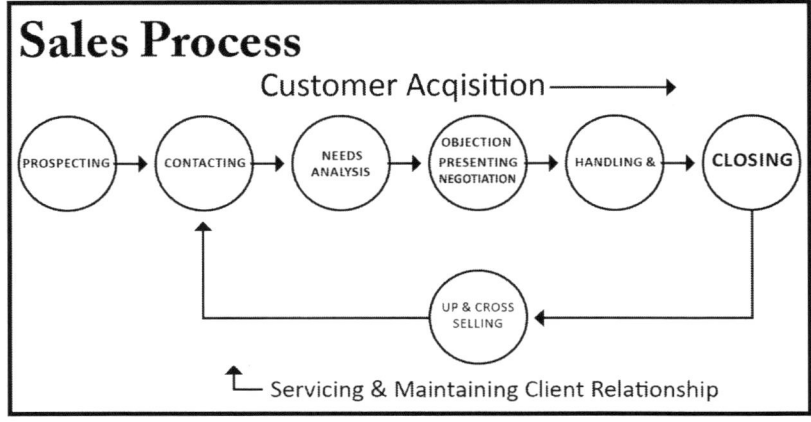

Handling Objections

For example, Julie's trucking company was able to zero in on a particular customer complaint from potential customers that she was calling on. They were all worried about late deliveries and are safety issues. Which makes sense, when you have paid for a crew and have construction permits and other sorts of huge project management logistics, a delayed delivery and safety problems can cost thousands of dollars – if not more. So, customers want their deliveries on time, every time without fail. Julie started focusing her sales by asking potential customers if their current vendor was providing them with on-time shipments and delivery of goods in a safe manner... if you are the potential customer and that's your biggest frustration, then hearing Julie and her salespeople ask that – you automatically think, 'Hey, these people know what the problem is! They get me!' Then Julie was able to answer those major pain points for the clients by walking them through their guaranteed delivery times and driver safety procedures they all followed.

Your first job to improve sales is to focus on finding the biggest frustrations that your potential clients are having right now and showing them that (1) you understand it and (2) you've come up with the proven solutions to make sure it isn't a problem ... as long as that potential customer becomes an actual customer.

Second is that process. Its process, process, process. If your salespeople have a process for handling objections (like when a potential customer says "This service costs too much" or when the food service director tells me just "drop it off with a brochure"), you need to make sure that each of your salespeople has access to the same best practices for how to respond to them.

Make Sure You are Selling the Right Service/Product to the Right Person

One of the biggest issues that I see is that entrepreneurs become so entrenched in what they are selling that they end up selling their product one way and often to only a few customers. So, let's say that you are one of these companies. Chances are that one of your best clients makes up 30-50% of your revenues. It's great that you have such a large client – but what if that one client takes their business elsewhere?

At any point, you don't want a single client in your portfolio to account for more than 10% of your business.

What happens when you have one giant client is that they almost end up holding your company over a barrel. They know how important their business is to you and they can ask things of you that you wouldn't give to any other client. Like a 10% decrease in price or asking for additional services that they aren't paying for – we call this "scope creep". The scope of the work you are doing gets bigger and bigger, but the fee seems to stay the same – so all that additional work (which could be thousands of dollars or even millions) is being done for free or at a lower price because the company becomes too worried about pushing them – in case they are fired. (Because if you get fired by the client that makes up 50% of your revenue, where are you left?)

Never put all your business eggs in one basket.

To fill these gaps, you need to always be selling.

There are simple ways of improving your sales to make sure that you aren't in a position like this – but you have to start thinking creatively. Pull together your dream team, that team of ten people from around the company and tell them you want to create a list of 100 ways that you can improve your sales. Direct the discussion with questions like: Are there other markets where we can sell into? Can we be more full service? How can we add more value and get paid for it?

Leverage Your Current Sales

Can we offer more than the one product that we are selling? For instance, if you have a heating and air conditioning company – you can sell a new air conditioning unit to a client. But how often does that client need a new air conditioning unit? Once every ten or twenty years? That's not bringing in new business. Imagine if you made it a more comprehensive, turn-key program? The client is already happy with your work and is already a customer of your company – how can you add to that a comprehensive service plan? Annual inspections, cleaning, service plans... something that brings in additional revenue every month as a sort of insurance coverage that goes beyond that initial sale.

What are other ancillary products that you can offer to the same client? An insurance plan that costs $20/mo. to make sure that they feel comfortable knowing that if anything happens to their system, your company will be out to fix it ... again, additional revenue beyond the initial sale.

I think that there is the perception of safety in small numbers. It's much easier to micromanage two roasted nut carts than it is to manage hundreds of locations – but if I only have two carts and one breaks down, what happens to my bottom line? If I have 50 locations and one breaks down, it won't impact me as roughly – and I might not even feel it.

Who Is Doing Your Sales?

If you have a sales team of three and a company of fifty plus people – why are you only empowering your sales people of three to go out and get new business? I have a client, an architectural firm, with three partners that are responsible for bringing in business – and yet they have 50 on staff. Imagine you had 50 people once a month go to some sort of networking event, meet contractors, real estate developers, or meet people interested in getting new projects done.

It becomes a networking opportunity where you've multiplied your sales force and were able to get your name out there by 50x. It takes additional planning and work, but the cost (in time and revenue) of empowering your employees to be your pseudo sales force is worth it!

Ready to refocus your
Sales Operations?
If you have not yet visited
www.theprofitpattern.com/bonus
(or Texted PROFIT to 58885)
be sure to!
There you will find a pdf that will help
you review the 3 primary pieces
of any business – How to:
Bring Business in (Sales),
Collect Monies and Pay Bills (Finance)
and Create Your Product or Service
(Operations)

"Quality means doing it right
when no one is looking."

–Henry Ford

CHAPTER 5

Get It Right
the First Time

Quality is one of the Top 10 most important ideals for your company – and more specifically, making sure that you get things right the first time. Rework, (having to do something more than once to get it right) can result in huge losses for most companies and it should be avoided at all costs. Let's say you manufacture bicycle frames. One department cuts the parts, another welds the frame together, another grinds the welds and another department paints the frame. The product isn't inspected each step of the way and arrives on the customer's doorstep – but when they open it up, something isn't right. Now you have an upset customer who will ship it back to you and then you have very expensive rework which is fixing a quality mistake or errors.

What does this do to your company? Well, first, those bikes are coming back – and you'll have to decide what to do with them. Scrap them? Cut them up and fix them? Regardless, your reputation is now in tatters with that client and if it has happened more than once, you're going to lose that client completely.

We are talking about making sure that the quality process is good and solid from start to finish. In the manufacturing example, you can have each department act as quality control for the previous department. The welder would check the previous department's cutting. The painting department would check that the welding is smooth... that way no particular product gets very far in the process before it's checked and rechecked. It's part of the process now and there won't be slips where some products fall through the cracks and make it to the customer without being checked.

Case Study: Gail Glasser - Century Fasteners and Machine

"High Quality, That's something I really needed to learn how to make work – the flow down of your employees, how they work, if something goes wrong right at the start – where do you catch it and make sure there are no errors later on? It's really the flow down system that helped me..."

Internal customer quality checks not only help reduce and even eliminate 'rework' (any work that you have to redo more than once in order to get it right), but it allows you, as a company, to pinpoint immediate problems in your process. This is a constant control feedback loop, and you'll be able to see where communication or quality is flagging and fix it quickly, with less work and less resources.

At the end of the day, your job is to deliver to the customer what they paid for and what they want. Being able to be consistent, internally, will help you do this in the most financially advantageous way possible.

Do you have a rework problem? Do you have quality control issues? If you are delivering late on projects, you've recently scrapped projects or if a customer is sending products back – then you have a quality control problem.

Quality doesn't only imply manufacturing, sometimes quality can be a sales problem or a project management problem. Let's say that you have given a quote for a particular client, the work will cost you $100 and you're charging $1000, but one week in, you've already logged the full amount of hours and you're only 1/10 done with the project... well, you have a quality issue.

Your project was either improperly scoped from the start, or mistakes and issues are causing the project to grow larger and not capturing the deliverables in the correct way.

Companies usually don't measure these types of things and yet question why they are reworking, scrapping, delivering late or getting things shipped back on a regular basis.

It's important for you to make sure that your quality at each step of the process (from planning to delivery) is meeting the standards that you've promised your customer.

Measuring Quality

Finding out how many times it takes you to do a project correctly isn't hard to track, and is your first key performance indicator (and one that you can improve upon and see a difference!). Tracking it from one department to the next, seeing where - in the process – things aren't meeting expectations is a great way of tracking quality by department.

But you can also track and measure quality by holding people accountable – ask them to measure the amount of waste, the value of the waste in time or resources and to come up with ways to continually minimize the waste moving forward. If this is the problem, ask them to sit down and come up with a solution and write it down and follow/test it for a month. Did things improve? Are the KPIs improving? If so, tweak again until it's running at an optimum level and then you have your Quality SOP.

In order to get people to take responsibility for their own part of the quality matrix, it's important to build an environment where people not only want to improve but, are also willing to admit the mistakes in the first place. Whether that's by marking something on a SOP checklist or discussing quality control issues during brainstorming sessions, creating a system where your employees can confidently (and without fear of reprisal) express their concerns or point out their own flaws/mistakes, then you're also empowering those employees to find their own solutions or –if they cannot – find someone who can help them find a solution with confidence.

Top 10 – Lack of Innovation

Innovation

/ɪnə'veɪʃ(ə)n/

noun
1. The action or process of innovating.
    "innovation is crucial to the continuing success of any organization"
    synonyms: **change, alteration, revolution,upheaval, transformation, metamorphosis**, reorganization, restructuring, rearrangement, recasting, remodelling, **renovation**, restyling, **variation; More**

I love talking about innovation. Jack Welch, of General Electric, once said something that rang so true for me – "if the rate of change outside your company is faster than the rate of change inside your company, the end is near". So innovation is critical for companies that want to succeed and grow.

Some companies manage not to make any changes for decades. Literally decades. Einstein once said the definition of insanity is "doing or saying the same thing over and over again and expecting different results", so what causes companies to think, "Hey, we're not growing, we're not profitable and we're having these challenges – but let's keep doing the same thing over and over and over and things will turn out OK."

It's not true.

Ultimately, the mindset of innovation within your company is critical and it starts at the top. It's not just about coming out with a new product or service, it's about finding ways to constantly do things better, faster, cheaper. But if you're going to become an innovative company, you're going to have to become comfortable with change. You're going to have to tuck away the fear of change (that we all know) and dig past that to the fear of losing your business. Which is worse?

My mantra for the entrepreneur is that you have to be like a tiger and be fearless at what you're doing. You have to change things or you'll never make progress. So, I ALWAYS ask myself simple questions:

- How can I do this better, cheaper and faster?
- How can I service my clients better?
- How do I make the process more efficient?

If I have ten customers standing in line at a roasted nut cart (and nobody likes standing in line) how can I make that process go a little faster or better for those ten customers? Start small, it's not about recreating the wheel – it's about making that wheel more efficient!

This is a mindset you have to cultivate in yourself and your company and continually feed. When I was looking at the roasted nut cart, originally you'd have to bend down, open the drawer, stick your head inside the cart and scoop up a bag of almonds and throw them in the roaster. It took a bit of time, so I augmented the cart to include a sliding drawer where you could simply pull it out and scoop. It saved time, made it easier (you didn't have to stick your head in the cart anymore) and made the entire process cheaper by virtue of less wasted time.

We don't have to fear innovation, because innovation doesn't mean that you have to start from scratch. Innovation can mean improving in small increments all the time.

Your job as an entrepreneur is to look at everything that you're doing and figure out small steps on making things a little better. It's an unbelievable challenge that you can accomplish a little each day – and it will make a huge impact on your bottom line.

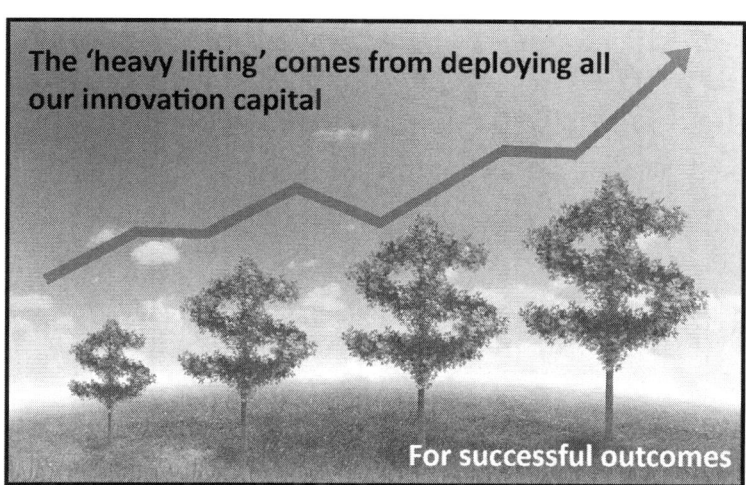

The 'heavy lifting' comes from deploying all our innovation capital

For successful outcomes

Challenge yourself and your employees to flex that innovation muscle — especially if your business is plateauing and not growing. That's a byproduct of a lack of innovation. Get your people to start thinking about something they can do right now that would create a better experience for their customer. Maybe it's something as small as moving a toolbox a little closer so that employees don't have to walk as far to access it. That's innovation!

One thing that I feel a lot of businesses hesitate to do is actually speak with their customers on how the process can be improved. It's scary, but it's scarier to never change and lose that client. So, let's say you get five of your customers in a room and ask them very direct questions:

- Why do you do business with us?
- What are things that we could do better?
- What are some innovative things that we could help you with and learn from?

Ask a series of searching questions, because they are the only ones that can actually answer you — asking these questions of your employees will still give you hypothetical answers. Maybe this is what the client wants. Maybe this is what the client likes... skip the hypotheticals and talk directly to the client.

This is also great for small or one-person companies. Your 5-10 person dream team can include clients and vendors and trusted resources such as your accountant, banker and lawyer, for example. You can pull together vendors that you buy products from and suddenly you have a small focus group. Try to figure out what you can do better from both a customer and vendor perspective and you'll be surprised as to what you can learn.

Innovation needs to start at the top, but that doesn't mean you can't get ideas from throughout your organization. You'll first want to make sure your employees are engaged; internal innovation gains the most traction. So, ask the people in your organization how you could create a better experience. Innovation isn't a one-time thing, it leads to other creative ideas, and it begs for tweaking and iteration, so any time that innovation works – great, build on that. But expect some failures, which are OK – because you will learn from those too.

A note for those who aren't sure they want to ask their employees for their help:

There are a lot of reasons to ask the people in your company for their opinion and there are only a few reasons not to do so – pride and fear. Let's talk about how (and why) you should phrase your invitation:

"We are all good at what we do – you are on the ground; I need your perspective."

Remember, you might be nervous about how your employees will react if you ask for their advice, but they are probably already nervous that you've called them "down to your office" to begin with! So, put them at ease right away by letting them know that they are there because they've done a good job – and that they can offer you a perspective that you can't receive elsewhere.

"I care about what you are thinking..."

Telling your employees that you care about their thoughts (and actually meaning it), is an amazing way of building trust and opening the lines of communication. Everyone has worked for someone else and had an idea of how the business could be improved. It's because when you are working a particular job, you become the expert on that position and you are the best person to suggest improvements! Your employees are in exactly the same position – so how, as a former employee, would you have wanted your suggestion greeted? With suspicion from upper management or with an open ear and an eye towards improvement for the greater whole?

Case Study: James Huckabee VP Star Detective Agency

"It's a challenge. You might feel embarrassed, scared or wonder if your ideas (or their ideas) are going to be any good – you are going to feel all that anxiety. And it's because you've never been taught that it was OK to participate in this sort of thing. The important thing to remember is that your employees feel the same way. They will be worried that they won't impress their boss or their peers, or they won't get rewarded or recognized for it – it takes a lot of patience to get people to do things they don't normally feel comfortable doing. But once you can help them make that initial leap, you'll see them meeting you more than halfway. They become more confident in sharing and opening up – as long as you are providing the right environment." – James, Vice President

One last word of caution – Suggestion boxes do NOT work. Don't try and skip over the "hard" parts of face to face interaction, by throwing up a box in the hallway. You'll get wonderful snack suggestions or we need to paint the bathroom green because it will make me feel better, but not the meaningful discourse that you'll receive by gathering ten people in a room to brainstorm together. It's a little more time consuming, it's a little tougher to manage than the old' suggestion box – but as they say, you get what you pay for.

Case Study: Trans International

Jaime and her sister Denise took over the family business, a freight audit payment company that had been started over 30 years earlier by their father. But it wasn't an easy transition – right away they had to deal with two major, demoralizing events in their organization: Jaime's uncle had recently had a debilitating stroke and had to leave his position as Vice President of the company – leaving a gaping hole in the upper management and in the company's continuity. The second issue was they had just finished dealing with large employee embezzlement. Two things that could knock the wind out of any small business owner and Jaime and her sister had to deal with both within months of taking over.

Soon after, the recession hit and they, as owners, had to cut back on the staff and salaries – and all the combined problems affected the morale of the company's employees. Jaime and her sister were dealing with growing frustrations that even as business began to pick up, it didn't feel like the motivation within their own halls was improving. "It was like no one gave a crap," Jaime recollects. "We had a staff that was slowly compensated and so to get them engaged in the business was a really difficult process for us."

As I started coaching Jaime, she didn't automatically take to the process that I set before her, she was resistant and enjoyed arguing with me – but she agreed to do an initial survey, and the results weren't pretty. They already knew that their employees weren't engaged, but their employees also felt that they weren't being communicated with and weren't being trained.

"They just felt like they weren't being heard. They felt like things were coming down from on high and none of it would be beneficial," explains Jaime. "They wanted to know why some people were held accountable for getting work done while other people weren't... they wanted to know why nobody was telling them when they were doing a good job."

Jaime selected her ten people "dream team" from a varied

list throughout the company. She selected a few highly capable people (those with high aptitude in their positions), as well as a few people from the middle and a few that she knew were going to be argumentative. But when everyone in the group made notes on what they thought could use improvement – the lists were very similar across the board.

It wasn't just the complainers, or the people who had been in the position a long time – but it was everyone – the new people, the highly efficient workers, they all saw the same problems. So we made a list and attached a dollar amount (how much value we thought we could bring to the company by making improvements in each area that was spotted) before we assembled teams of employees and managers to tackle each of these problems.

The teams would go and work and then report back weekly on progress, but otherwise Jaime and her sister were not involved or in control of the process – the employees were.

"So they're in control of this process. I mean we guide it and tell them whether or not we think they're on or off the right path, and try to keep them on task. And it's kind of fun because when we come into the room, all of our hats are off - all of our titles and egos are kind of checked at the door. I liked that they started feeling comfortable challenging us and making us think about things in a different way. And now we've got people signing up for tiger teams, signing up for the steering committee to get on it when there are openings and we're just really moving the needle on projects. And some of these projects have really big ROI's attached to them."

Here are some fun and amazing ways that Jaime has incorporated employee suggestions into the everyday business practices of her organization:

- "We would keep silly string on every employee's desk, and if somebody was getting angry or too serious they would do that. They would like pull out the silly string because, I mean, why are you getting angry about something that is not going to matter in 300 years? This is not significant stuff. There's no reason for you to stress yourself out about it."

- "The CEO and the COO would get together in a room and employees can just come in and ask us anything. Anything they want about the company, about your personal lives, about our philosophy on life, whatever it is. And so we started having these sessions once a month to try to get people to talk to each other to get to know us better. To get to know why we're doing this, and what our vision is for the company."

- "We have our CMO – our Chief Morale Officer. It's a volunteer position and if there are too many volunteers, there is a company vote as to who is going to be the Chief Morale Officers, and they're given a budget, and they can plan just mini- activities. So instead of throwing all this money at one big company event, like to go to a Brewer game or something, we have chunked it out into little events all year long, and let the CMO's have complete control over that."

Jaime believes that they were able to turn around the morale of the company in about six months – and were able to reinforce the "turn around" by showing it in bonuses that were based on company performance. A year after the initial survey, we gave Jaime's employees a second survey.

"We had a 110% improvement in our scores. It was amazing."

What are the 7 most important questions
when it comes to ingraining QUALITY
in your company culture?
Find out by visiting:
www.theprofitpattern.com/bonus
or by texting PROFIT to 58885.

"Happiness is a positive cash flow."

–Fred Adler

CHAPTER 6

The Lifeblood
of Every Company

Cash flow is the lifeblood of your company. Basically – if you run out of cash, you run out of business and cannot exist. It's a constant problem, because most entrepreneurs focus on income coming in, expenses going out and then the bottom line of profit. But, you can be profitable and still have a cash flow problem.

Cash flow is the flow of money in and out of the company. Let's say that we're back in the bike manufacturing business again and you received a huge order for Christmas from a big box retailer. Your bottom line is that you have sales, you have money coming in, you have expenses going out – but if that big box retailer doesn't pay you on time, your receivables could be causing you a lot of heartache in the cash flow arena. You could potentially have to close your business before you ever receive the payment, because you didn't have enough in the bank to keep the lights on.

Often, companies do not say anything when having to deal with a good customer that is slow to pay. They just hope that it comes in, they do not want to rattle the cage and say 'we are 90 days late on payment', because they are afraid they will upset their customer. I think for companies that are really focusing on improving their cash flow, they have to look at their collection procedures to make sure their receivables are coming in. What do you do with the customer that is beyond 90 days late because they are dragging their feet and its 6 months on? In the meanwhile, you have had to pay your employees, the rent and other expenses and yet this customer is taking 6 months to pay you. How do you handle situations and get cash to come in properly?

Having a one million dollar in sales company is great, unless that money isn't in your account – but still out there in the pockets of your customers.

Lack of standard operating procedures can be a root causal issue of having cash flow problems because people are doing things differently each time - there is a lack of consistency. Other root causal issues of cash flow could be lack of a good quality control system, which can cause things like scrap, waste, rework, overtime, later deliveries, expedited shipments, errors on paperwork, not getting it right the first time, all that wasted time, movement and types of things.

Cash flow can be the symptom of a root cause issue like quality. When I talk about a symptom and root cause, if you had a dandelion in your yard growing as weed, it popped up and you took your lawn mower and cut it off, what is going to happen a week later? Normally a week later that dandelion will pop back up, maybe even spread the seed around and you might have 20 more dandelions. The reason it popped up out the ground again is because cutting it off with the lawn mower is not going to solve the problem, it grew back because there is a root you did not get. Until we get to the root of the issue that dandelion is going to keep coming back up again and again. Cash flow can be a symptomatic issue of other thing such as: quality, scheduling, lack of standard operating procedures, communication problems, bidding, and project scope changes, returned orders or estimating issues.

To really look at cash flow and manage it as a juggling act all the time, can be very stressful constantly. I think business owners are invariably juggling cash constantly. I can say that it is a wonderful thing when you have money in the bank, your receivables are coming in because you have quality in the work you are doing, no upset customers or delays, you are having a good collection process and managing your expenses better, you are smart in terms of when you get your payments out the door and various things like that. It can be so nice to have positive cash flow. It is a life changing experience when someone does not have to be under the gun every week trying to make ends meet. They sense it but they do not really understand how to get above and beyond it as an issue.

When I decided to invest almost a million dollars in the roasted nut carts in order to open up many new locations in one year, I bit off more than I could chew. I had a real cash flow problem: I could not pay the bills for a period of time until those carts were up and running – and my investment money wasn't paying off yet.

With a lust for quick expansion like that you can literally grow yourself out of business especially if you run out of money or if your projections were incorrect.

Another problem you need to keep an eye out for is customers with cash flow problems – if your customer is having a cash flow problem, so are you. Let's say you have a big customer that owes you $400,000 and you are counting on that money to pay your bills, buy a new truck, etc. If your customer is slow to pay, they might be in trouble, in which case, your chances of getting the money they owe you greatly diminishes with each passing day.

Take a look at the customers you extend credit to and make sure they are solvent – or you may never see that money. For new customers, you'll want to get familiar with their payment history before extending them large amounts of credit on big projects so, ask for deposits if possible.

Accounts Receivable

To improve your accounts receivable, your best practices will include getting those invoices out the door early and often – maybe even providing a discount if they pay early (some companies will definitely take advantage of a 2% paid in 10 days' approach). Maybe there are some sort of incentives you can use to get those payments in – because we're focused on cash in hand, not cash in theory.

The other thing you can do to improve cash flow is to extend payments to vendors. Instead of sending a company a check for $20,000, maybe you can arrange to send them $5,000 a week for 4 weeks. Even though you could make the payment at once, why do that if you can manage your cash flow a bit better?

Often, when cash flow gets ugly, I think we end up getting scared and hide, hoping it gets better. But what ultimately happens it that your vendors are waiting for you to pay them and they don't know what's going on. It's much better to be upfront and forthright, saying something like, "In the 20-year history of our company, this is the first time we are experiencing a cash crunch. I really want to be completely upfront with you, and make sure you get paid every nickel that is owed to you because we have always been able to pay you and want to keep our relationship strong. Can you continue to extend us terms or can we come up with a payment plan right now?"

The best policy is to be upfront and honest! Everyone needs to get paid and this will go a long way to making sure that you don't burn any bridges between you, your customers and your vendors.

Positive cash flow can be a life-changing experience and, over time, when people deal with negative or slow cash flow, sometimes they think that is the world I live in and it cannot get any better. But it can get better if you take some direct action and you almost grab the challenge head on and confront it. Also as I say, look at those operational things in your business, quality procedures, bidding in the estimating process scheduling, managing your inventories, all of those things can make a big difference in helping you manage and get better cash flow.

Ways to Improve

Get a list of your receivables – who owes you money right now? Come up with a plan for getting that money through your front door. Take a look at your expenses over the next four weeks and do a cash flow projection of what your payments are going to be moving forward over the next four weeks, looking four weeks at a time.

Figure out what you have to put out over the next four weeks and then what expected payments you have coming in.

This will give you a broad view as to what's going out the

door and what's coming in, so you can start juggling things around and say, "I do not think I'll have my rent next week – maybe I need to call the landlord and ask if I can pay a week late." Moving that payment to the following week should free up some cash.

You can literally manage your cash flow week-by-week, or month-by-month.

A problem with Cash Flow
can be a problem with your business'
very existence! Use our simple yet
impactful quiz to discover if you have a
reporting problem and providing
ideas on **how to fix it**. Visit:
www.theprofitpattern.com/bonus
or Text *PROFIT* to 58885
to access this critical quiz.

"Progress is impossible without change and those who cannot change their minds cannot change anything."

–George Bernard Shaw

CHAPTER 7

The Balance of
Not Enough or Too Much

There are so many companies that live and die by their inventory controls that it's impossible to not include this on the list. Manufacturing, restaurants, warehouses, distributors, retail companies...all of these companies grapple with how to control inventory which means controlling profitability.

I worked with a construction company, where I sat down with the owners as they wanted to figure out how they were going to get a handle on all of their inventory in the yard.

They had hundreds of thousands of dollars in tubing, piping, fiber optic cables and wires as well as trucks, sheds, garages and all sorts of other equipment required to do underground construction work. They even had extra equipment for when machines would break down! Improving the inventory for this company could mean a tremendous opportunity in really improving the profitability.

We started by focusing on the concept of organization – we want our inventory to mimic a Chef's kitchen. Imagine a kitchen where all the pots and pans are organized, everything is placed in the most efficient position – all the knives and spoons are ready for use and within arm's reach – now compare this to a messy garage that had everything, all over the place. That's the discrepancy we were trying to bridge.

The first step was to differentiate between the things worth keeping, worth selling and the things worth nothing – so we had a team that would break things into piles: things that were to be thrown out, things that could be sold or scrapped and things that needed to be logged and placed somewhere for future use. After a while, we realized that it was not a sustainable situation – we had things everywhere. The tool and truck repair garage manager would have needed some brake pads and would go buy a box of them only to find out later that we already had six boxes of them hidden in the back of the storage area. We needed to clean up, clean out and make a committed rule to make no further purchases until we were sure that we didn't already have something in stock.

Next, we had to get better shelving – as every item needed its own place. We had enough inventory for about two years, so we didn't have to buy anything. We were able to move some things really quickly (like things with two or more inches of dust). But we slowly made headway, we were able to label and compartmentalize products, put in indicators that signaled to managers when items had to be reordered and started saving space and room by getting their trucks in and out faster and in a more organized fashion.

How do you know if you have an Inventory Problem?

- Can you tell me what you've got in inventory right now?
- Is there a report you can show me that explains exactly what you have, where it is and what it is worth?
- Do you spend more money on inventory being overnighted to you in order to support your business needs?
- Is some of your inventory literally rotting or walking out the back door?

Answer yes to any of these questions and you probably have an inventory problem.

The construction company was trying to decide if they could live with literally zero inventory, so I asked them questions, "How fast can you get tires? How fast can you get brake pads? How fast can you get drills?" So, getting into "just in time inventory" is a powerful thing. It's when you have just enough on the shelf for maybe the next 24 hours — but you allow your supplier/vendor to carry the inventory knowing you can get more within 24 hours.

You need to have a clear understanding of how long it takes to get something, how long it will last, how much you need the item? But most companies don't need all the inventory they hold and it's important for your bottom line not to carry six months' worth of supplies that you only need one day's worth of supply.

Changing your inventory management will greatly impact your cash flow — which will greatly impact your company's profitability.

Avoid Hoarder Mentality

There is a particular hoarder mindset that I see a lot. Let's say you've held onto a specific part for three years and the day after you get rid of it, a client calls and asks for that particular part but you can't sell it to them because you just got rid of it. That is why some companies never throw things away. It's actually something based in fear, hoarding for the potential of some lost business – when it makes sense to get rid of your unused inventory and use that cash and space for something else that will better benefit your organization.

My guess - there are several things
in this chapter that will change
your business 'today'!
To gain access to our
Controlling Your Inventory pdf,
created especially for you,
visit the membership site:
www.theprofitpattern.com/bonus
or Text *PROFIT* to 58885
to receive this amazing report that
will create an immediate impact
on your bottom line.

"People with goals succeed because they know where they are going... It's as simple as that."

–Earl Nightingale

CHAPTER 8

What Goes Together Like Peanut Butter and Jelly?

Another top ten, is project management. If you find that your company ends up doing a lot of additional work for free because you're not keeping clear track of change orders or scope creep, then you probably have a project management issue.

First, you'll want to deal with the scope of the project – great time management will help get a project done on time and on budget. But also managing the process throughout the time you have allotted will save your company money and make your projects more profitable. Let's say that you have a 100-hour project, five days to do it in, and three days are gone – but you've used 80 hours of the 100 and now any hours that you run over on this project are basically being written off by your company (i.e. you're not making money on them!). Keeping a close eye on the hours you are spending and the work being produced and balancing them is what project management is all about.

Can you keep track of what his happening through accurate reporting? If you don't, how can you know if your project is on track, if you've properly quoted your client, if you're losing or making money?

Each job that you do can be broken down into particular phases and tasks, allotted to different codes and time that can then be tracked with some basic time tracking software.

Project Management is very similar to preparing a four-course meal for ten people that needs to be ready at 7pm. How does it all happen at the same time, for all the food to make it to the table – warm, but not burned and in the right progression? We need some way of tracking how long each item will take to make and then plan it backward from the 7pm delivery. The same goes for a 10-week architectural project – the first activity is to make sure that everything is ready to go and then chart the different steps of the project so that you know that you'll be ending at the right time.

Pulling a small group together to talk about the scope of the project, what's involved and what each department has to do in order to make it a success will minimize confusion and make sure that everyone is on board with what has to happen to make the project a success. The project manager's job is to make sure that this is all documented and then enforced (just like the SOP!).

That way if there are changes to the project (like if a client wants to enlarge her kitchen by four feet – and then the architectural renderings need to be redone, the scope of work has changed), you'll have a clear idea of how much additional work needs to be done to make the project a success for the client, but you'll also know how much to charge the client for the scope change.

If you are doing project based work of any sort and are dealing with scope creep that you aren't billing your client for – then your projects are not coming out as profitable as you thought, they would be and you have a project management problem. Tracking these changes could save you thousands of dollars. Isn't that worth the effort?

One of the things a company can do is take a look at the last three jobs that they've bid on and say what did we bid it for? If you bid for 10% profit check to see if you actually made that profit. You might be unpleasantly surprised by the percentage of profit you actually did (or didn't) make.

A post-wrap up meeting, after the project is completed, is also really important and they should be used to review projects, how well they were completed, what problems arose and how the successes can be duplicated.

5 Tips on Improving Your Project Management Today

Tip 1: Nail Down the Details

Make sure that you really understand the details of the project you are about to get into, the key elements, the entire scope and make sure there are measurable outcomes that you can track. Not knowing (or not having a clear idea) of each step, means that you cannot really judge the profitability of that project and therefore won't know if you're making money or not.

Tip 2: Get the Team Requirements Together

Once you have a clear plan, you'll want to start getting the players together - and assign someone to be the project manager. This person should be a good leader, be able to hold people accountable and move things along as necessary.

Tip 3: Have A Good Idea of Your Critical Project Milestones

By the end of week 1, 4, 9… where should we be? If you don't know where you're headed, you'll never get there. Have a good idea of where you should be at critical milestones and then you know where you are headed.

Tip 4: Communicate, Communicate and Communicate Some More!

Do not keep your team or your clients in the dark – let them know how things are progressing. Be open and honest with issues and no project will ever get so far down the rabbit hole that it cannot be saved.

Tip 5: Evaluate

What lessons were learned? What were the disappointments or victories – and how do we keep doing the things we did well? Here are the things you want to talk about at the end of the product, to make sure that you are learning from your mistakes and adding your successes to your best practices.

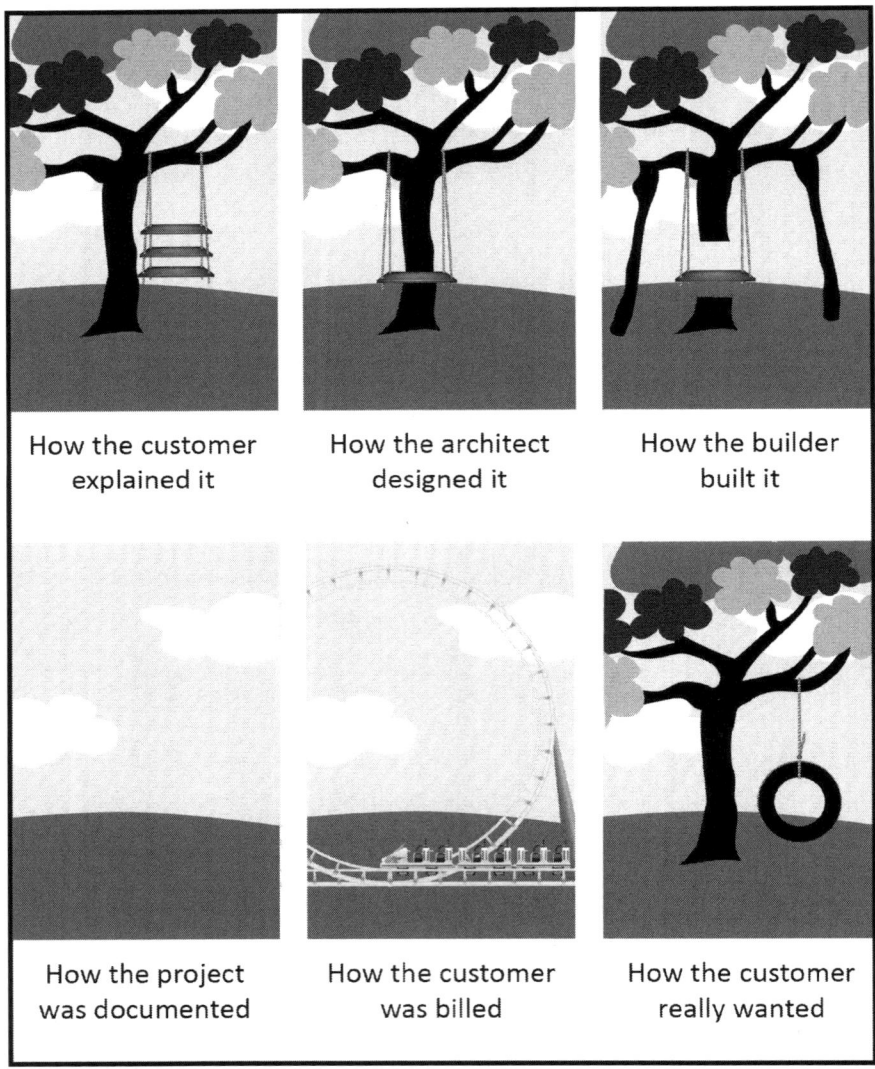

Ready to minimize overtime
in your organization?
With proper planning you can
effectively minimize overtime.
When you visit our special
membership site:
www.theprofitpattern.com/bonus
(or Text *PROFIT* to 58885)
we have a mini-report on job management.
Here you will find the formula
to answer the big question –
How do I minimize overtime?

"If you're not gonna go all the way, why go at all?"

–Joe Namath

CHAPTER 9

Let's Play a Game That You Can Never Win

'll give you a dollar and you give me a dollar and 5 cents back. And let's repeat this over and over one million times. Crazy right? Some people believe in doing this because they can make it up in volume, wrong!

I worked with a manufacturing company where 30% of their sales came from one account – but after looking at this one account they realized that they were losing a small percentage of money every year on shipping product and servicing this client. They went to the client and explained the situation. They told them that they loved doing business with them, they simply couldn't find any way to be more efficient and they were losing money on the relationship. The client told them too bad, take it or leave it.

Ultimately, the company had to let the client go – they went from a 100 million in sales to 70 million in sales, but by getting rid of that one unprofitable customer that was not willing to work with them or change their pricing structure, they became a profitable 70-million-dollar company.

Sometimes taking a clear view of your accounts and eliminating unprofitable customers can be a good thing – and looking at the way you bid is the first natural step in that process.

First, you need to keep in mind that you can bid yourself into failure as a business – your first question needs to be, should I be chasing this work in the first place? Companies should not try to be everything to everyone, nor should you bid on every work that comes across your desk. You need to analyze the situation based on factual data – like have we made money the last time we did this? Is this something we can do profitably? Can we offer a great customer experience and price and still make a profit? Have labor or material-related expenses gone up recently?

Sometimes it makes sense not to bid.

Another bidding quandary that happens all the time is when a company loses a $50,000 bid by a small amount – like $500. What that signals is a customer that is price shopping, but in reality, you get what you pay for and a customer who is in the business to nickel and dime you for everything, who will be slow to pay, is not the kind of relationship you want with another company. If you can create a partnership so that both sides benefit and can sustain those benefits together, then you have a good reason to do business together.

The lowest price is rarely ever the lowest price. Explain to your customer that there is a reason you charge what you do – "there will be less problems further downstream, we will get things right the first time, we have years more experience, we know what we are doing, we are going to be solving your problems and offering better solutions."

You have to take this philosophy that you have to bid for profit, otherwise do not do the work. Having said that, it could be a situation where you are going to come in as a low price, thinking that maybe over time I will increase my prices, I will come in, we will do this job for $30,000, I know that if I do this I will probably break-even but I know it is a way to get an in with this big company that I can do business with. I bet the next job I get I am going to bid $40,000 and I can make $10,000 profit.

The problem with that philosophy is that they are not going to do that, they are going to say wait a minute the last time we did this it was 30 now why is it 40? In a way you have locked yourself into this lower price and there is price resistance, the customers are going to want to question why are you raising the price all the time?

One of the first things I ask my clients is when was the last time they raised their rates or prices. If it's been more than a year or two, I point out that the price of living has gone up, that expenses have gone up and probably things like payroll or materials have also risen. So when you're a ten-million-dollar company a small increase can generate a lot of additional profit – and if you let your clients know, they generally don't push back on you if it's presented in a logical professional way, and if they are happy with the work that you are already doing.

How Can You Tell If You Are Having a Bidding Issue?

TYPES OF ERRORS
CARELESS ERROR
Writing the Wrong Number | Not Following Directions
COMPUTATION ERROR
Adding, Subtracting, Multiplying, or Dividing Incorrectly
PRECISION ERROR
Work Too Messy to Understand | Dropping a Negative Sign | Forgetting Parentheses
Missing Units | Lack of Labeling | Incorrect Notation
PROBLEM SOLVING ERROR
Not Following Rules of Algebra | Failure to Complete all of the Steps
Not Showing Thinking for Each Step

Take a look at your top ten customers and figure out your profit margins for each. Usually you will find a variance between which customers you make more profit on and those you do not. If you find a particular project type that you bid on doesn't make much profit – that might be one of the types of bids you don't make anymore (or raise your bid on).

Remember that you should not win every bid (if so, you're pricing way too low). You should be aiming to win between 20 to 30% of the bids you make.

Would you like to receive Tips and Techniques on Better Bidding? We'd love to share them with you so you can see an immediate impact on your business. Just visit our website:
www.theprofitpattern.com/bonus
or text PROFIT to 58885.

"All communication problems are due to
the reason that we don't listen to understand.
We listen only to reply!"

–Unknown

CHAPTER 10

Seek to Understand,
Then Be Understood

Poor communication can be very expensive. Lack of clear communication from top down, bottom up, department to department, to and from customers, not having clear goals and time management can be very costly. Communication problem often occur from the office to the field and field to the office. Construction companies for instance, get this wrong all the time because, the workers in the field hate doing the paperwork, keeping reports updated or calling at the end of the day. This can be very costly with change order not being tracked, project scope creep growing and problems not being communicated.

Often lack of organizational structure is one of the main issues of poor communications, and everyone would go right to the top of the company for answers or direction and that can become confusing and stressful for the person at the top. Lack of communication is almost like vapor, you cannot touch it or feel it, it is like air, and you know it is around you but it is not tangible in a way.

I feel that there are a number of ways to look at communication in a company. Thinking of communication as either 1-way communication or 2-way communication, how do you communicate with others, how does the organization communicate its information to its people and get information coming back in?

One of the biggest challenges in communication is because of poor listening – with the key rule being that you should always be listening twice as much as you are talking in order to be an effective communicator. You have one mouth and two ears so use that as a guide to the amount of listening vs. talking.   I've been guilty of this as well. Sometimes you feel like you know or can anticipate where a conversation is heading, so to save time, and you cut the person off and jump in with a response. Focusing on listening allows you to get a really good sense of the actual problem (not the perceived problem), plus, it won't damage the morale of your employees!

I find that the best method of communicating is still picking up the phone or going to see someone to speak about the challenge. It may take five or ten minutes, but it can save hours of time in writing emails that may not even fully express the challenges and issues.

It's a clear sign of poor communication if you ever find yourself yelling orders across the office – it causes poor morale, creates a poor work environment and makes people feel disrespected. But, with companies that have a higher morale and better work environment making them more productive, it's in your best interest (and the best interest of your company) to protect your employees – even from your own poor communication skills.

First, think of company meetings as being important – face to face meetings are critical as only 7% of communication is spoken and the other 93% is tone and body language. Five minute stand up meetings are highly effective ways to review challenges and issues and make sure people feel heard. These are primarily to share important and pertinent information on what's happening that day – all other topic should be discussed at another time.

If we are going to solve problems in those meetings and need to speak to the challenges that we are facing.

How to Structure Your Meetings

Meetings should be highly structured so that they don't waste time – because a meeting that wastes time will be the bane of everyone's existence (and as the meetings get more and more annoying for your employees – they will become less and less productive!). There are "5 rules" that you need to keep in mind for every meeting:

1- Start with something positive.
2- Discuss the positive thing/event/item – how did we do it? How do we keep doing it? (You're looking for ways to repeat successes)
3- Discuss specific areas that need to be improved (general discussion) and possible solutions.
4- Make decisions IN THE MEETING.
5- Set assignments, goals and timelines to review at the next meeting.

There are only three different kinds of meetings that you need in your company –

A Daily 5-Minute Standup

Every department should have a five-minute stand-up meeting where they have a quick rundown (given by one person) of the top most important details/projects for the day, just to outline what is happening that day. Further conversations and questions happen outside of the meeting. This is just to make sure everyone is on the same page.

Weekly Department Meeting

Once a week gather your department to discuss what is going well (and how to keep it going), possible improvements and then make decisions. Keep these meetings short, direct and decisive.

Monthly Executive Meeting

Once a month gather high-level management and discuss the financials, how the company performed since the last meeting, where you are headed and all positive and negative impacts upon the company within the past 30 days.

This will give everyone in your company a very clear idea of what is happening, what is working, what isn't and keep it on the forefront of their minds. This is also how you get your employees to start thinking about their positions and their company as being open to change and improvement.

Creating a great communication plan amongst your company is what will help your company identify solutions (the best solutions)!

Communication is key!
When you access the
special membership site:
www.theprofitpattern.com/bonus
or Text PROFIT to 58885,
my favorite tips on managerial reporting
for more effective communication
is waiting for you. It's short, easy to
implement and will change the way
you do business forever.

SOME FINAL THOUGHTS

OK, now you have the Top 10 Tools, so let's see how it might be affecting your profitability. This simple 12-question test gives a glimpse, based upon your perceptions, of the "Profitability Health" in your business. It won't give you dollar amounts, but it will give you an idea whether there is profit leaking out of your business. Please answer Yes or No to these issues, and, if the answer is "Yes", then rate your satisfaction from 0% (not satisfied) to 100 % (totally satisfied). Start working on the 3 that need to be improved the most.

Questions	No	Yes	Rating
Over the past year has your management actively tried to increase the profit level in the company?			
Do you know the average productivity per person of your company? (Sales / # Employees)			
During your standard reporting period do you measure the utilization of your non-personnel resources?			
Do you have a standardized and integrated planning process throughout your company?			
Can you accurately identify the value of the current inventory from raw goods to finished product?			
Have you had a review of your written Standard Operating Procedures in the past three months?			
Do you spend less than 10% of your time "fighting fires" that should have been handled at a different level?			
In the last six months, has cash flow been so tight that you've had to tap into your line-of-credit or other funding?			
Are your managers measured against written, pre-established operational goals?			
Do you consistently forecast and then deliver the profit margin on each of your products and for each of your customers?			
Does each position in your company have a clear, written, training plan?			
In the past month have you held any focused action team meetings improving specific problems?			

We know sometimes people don't like to write inside their book! So we have this simple 12 question analysis quiz in pdf format, waiting for you to print, inside our special membership site.

To access visit:

www.theprofitpattern.com/bonus
or Text *PROFIT* to 58885.

ABOUT THE AUTHOR

JOHN MAUTNER is a dreamer, doer and serial entrepreneur. His strategies and principles helped him launch five successful companies over the past 25 years.

Inc. Magazine awarded his first business he started at age 26, an Inc. 500 winner and one of America's 500 fastest growing companies. In an effort to help the countless struggling small to mid-sized companies' turnaround, grow faster and help entrepreneurs realize their dreams, John founded in 2001, the first and only business success program of its type: Cycle-of-Success Institute or COSi www.learncosi.com. Thousands of business owners, managers and employees across the US have learned COSi resulting in enhanced profitability, faster growth and creating winning workplace culture.

John has become an in-demand speaker and acknowledged specialist in the small business world and he knows what it takes to build a successful high growth company.

John has presented high impact workshops to thousands of business leaders across the country on; How to build a profitable high growth company that consistently produces exceptional results.

In addition to founding COSi, John hosted a live talk radio show in Chicago "Small Business Talk," has been featured in MS-NBC, Yahoo Finance, Entrepreneur Magazine, is a past member of the USA Today Small Business Panel and the past Illinois Honorary Chairman for the U.S. Department of Commerce Small Business Committee.

You can learn more about him and the Profit Pattern by visiting his website: www.JohnMautner.com

Printed in Great Britain
by Amazon